Gratitude Journal for Couples

Copyright © 2018 Art Book Publishing. All rights reserved. No part of this publication may be reproduced, distributed, or transmitted, in any form or by any means, including photocopying, recording, or other electronic or mechanical methods, without prior written permission of the publisher, except in the case of brief quotations embodied in critical reviews and certain other noncommercial uses permitted by copyright law.

Gratitude
changes everything.

- I AM THANKFUL FOR… DATE:
  1.
  2.
  3.

- I AM THANKFUL FOR… DATE:
  1.
  2.
  3.

- I AM THANKFUL FOR… DATE:
  1.
  2.
  3.

- I AM THANKFUL FOR ···   DATE:
    1.
    2.
    3.

- I AM THANKFUL FOR ···   DATE:
    1.
    2.
    3.

- I AM THANKFUL FOR ···   DATE:
    1.
    2.
    3.

- I AM THANKFUL FOR ···   • DATE:
    1.
    2.
    3.

Gratitude unlocks the fullness of life.
What are you grateful for this week?

Gratitude
changes everything.

- I AM THANKFUL FOR...   DATE:
    1.
    2.
    3.

- I AM THANKFUL FOR...   DATE:
    1.
    2.
    3.

- I AM THANKFUL FOR...   DATE:
    1.
    2.
    3.

- I AM THANKFUL FOR···   DATE:
1.
2.
3.

- I AM THANKFUL FOR···   DATE:
1.
2.
3.

- I AM THANKFUL FOR···   DATE:
1.
2.
3.

- I AM THANKFUL FOR···   - DATE:
1.
2.
3.

Gratitude unlocks the fullness of life.
What are you grateful for this week?

Gratitude
changes everything.

- **I AM THANKFUL FOR...** DATE:
  1.
  2.
  3.

- **I AM THANKFUL FOR...** DATE:
  1.
  2.
  3.

- **I AM THANKFUL FOR...** DATE:
  1.
  2.
  3.

- I AM THANKFUL FOR…   DATE:
  1.
  2.
  3.

- I AM THANKFUL FOR…   DATE:
  1.
  2.
  3.

- I AM THANKFUL FOR…   DATE:
  1.
  2.
  3.

- I AM THANKFUL FOR…   • DATE:
  1.
  2.
  3.

Gratitude unlocks the fullness of life.
What are you grateful for this week?

Gratitude
changes everything

- I AM THANKFUL FOR···   DATE:
  1.
  2.
  3.

- I AM THANKFUL FOR···   DATE:
  1.
  2.
  3.

- I AM THANKFUL FOR···   DATE:
  1.
  2.
  3.

- I AM THANKFUL FOR…   DATE:
1.
2.
3.

- I AM THANKFUL FOR…   DATE:
1.
2.
3.

- I AM THANKFUL FOR…   DATE:
1.
2.
3.

- I AM THANKFUL FOR…   • DATE:
1.
2.
3.

Gratitude unlocks the fullness of life.
What are you grateful for this week?

Gratitude
changes everything.

- **I AM THANKFUL FOR…**   DATE:
  1.
  2.
  3.

- **I AM THANKFUL FOR…**   DATE:
  1.
  2.
  3.

- **I AM THANKFUL FOR…**   DATE:
  1.
  2.
  3.

- I AM THANKFUL FOR···   DATE:
1.
2.
3.

- I AM THANKFUL FOR···   DATE:
1.
2.
3.

- I AM THANKFUL FOR···   DATE:
1.
2.
3.

- I AM THANKFUL FOR···   - DATE:
1.
2.
3.

Gratitude unlocks the fullness of life.
What are you grateful for this week?

Gratitude
changes everything

- **I AM THANKFUL FOR···** DATE:
  1.
  2.
  3.

- **I AM THANKFUL FOR···** DATE:
  1.
  2.
  3.

- **I AM THANKFUL FOR···** DATE:
  1.
  2.
  3.

- I AM THANKFUL FOR…   DATE:
  1.
  2.
  3.

- I AM THANKFUL FOR…   DATE:
  1.
  2.
  3.

- I AM THANKFUL FOR…   DATE:
  1.
  2.
  3.

- I AM THANKFUL FOR…   • DATE:
  1.
  2.
  3.

Gratitude unlocks the fullness of life.
What are you grateful for this week?

Gratitude
changes everything.

- **I AM THANKFUL FOR…**   DATE:
  1.
  2.
  3.

- **I AM THANKFUL FOR…**   DATE:
  1.
  2.
  3.

- **I AM THANKFUL FOR…**   DATE:
  1.
  2.
  3.

- I AM THANKFUL FOR···   DATE:
1.
2.
3.

- I AM THANKFUL FOR···   DATE:
1.
2.
3.

- I AM THANKFUL FOR···   DATE:
1.
2.
3.

- I AM THANKFUL FOR···   - DATE:
1.
2.
3.

Gratitude unlocks the fullness of life.
What are you grateful for this week?

Gratitude
changes everything.

- I AM THANKFUL FOR...   DATE:
  1.
  2.
  3.

- I AM THANKFUL FOR...   DATE:
  1.
  2.
  3.

- I AM THANKFUL FOR...   DATE:
  1.
  2.
  3.

- I AM THANKFUL FOR ···   DATE:
  1.
  2.
  3.

- I AM THANKFUL FOR ···   DATE:
  1.
  2.
  3.

- I AM THANKFUL FOR ···   DATE:
  1.
  2.
  3.

- I AM THANKFUL FOR ···   • DATE:
  1.
  2.
  3.

Gratitude unlocks the fullness of life.
What are you grateful for this week?

- I AM THANKFUL FOR··· DATE:

1.
2.
3.

- I AM THANKFUL FOR··· DATE:

1.
2.
3.

- I AM THANKFUL FOR··· DATE:

1.
2.
3.

- I AM THANKFUL FOR ··· DATE:
    1.
    2.
    3.

- I AM THANKFUL FOR ··· DATE:
    1.
    2.
    3.

- I AM THANKFUL FOR ··· DATE:
    1.
    2.
    3.

- I AM THANKFUL FOR ··· • DATE:
    1.
    2.
    3.

Gratitude unlocks the fullness of life.
What are you grateful for this week?

Gratitude
changes everything.

- **I AM THANKFUL FOR...** DATE:
  1.
  2.
  3.

- **I AM THANKFUL FOR...** DATE:
  1.
  2.
  3.

- **I AM THANKFUL FOR...** DATE:
  1.
  2.
  3.

- I AM THANKFUL FOR…   DATE:
  1.
  2.
  3.

- I AM THANKFUL FOR…   DATE:
  1.
  2.
  3.

- I AM THANKFUL FOR…   DATE:
  1.
  2.
  3.

- I AM THANKFUL FOR…   • DATE:
  1.
  2.
  3.

Gratitude unlocks the fullness of life.
What are you grateful for this week?

- I AM THANKFUL FOR...   DATE:
  1.
  2.
  3.

- I AM THANKFUL FOR...   DATE:
  1.
  2.
  3.

- I AM THANKFUL FOR...   DATE:
  1.
  2.
  3.

- I AM THANKFUL FOR···   DATE:
  1.
  2.
  3.

- I AM THANKFUL FOR···   DATE:
  1.
  2.
  3.

- I AM THANKFUL FOR···   DATE:
  1.
  2.
  3.

- I AM THANKFUL FOR···   • DATE:
  1.
  2.
  3.

Gratitude unlocks the fullness of life.
What are you grateful for this week?

Gratitude
changes everything.

- I AM THANKFUL FOR...   DATE:
    1.
    2.
    3.

- I AM THANKFUL FOR...   DATE:
    1.
    2.
    3.

- I AM THANKFUL FOR...   DATE:
    1.
    2.
    3.

- I AM THANKFUL FOR…   DATE:
  1.
  2.
  3.

- I AM THANKFUL FOR…   DATE:
  1.
  2.
  3.

- I AM THANKFUL FOR…   DATE:
  1.
  2.
  3.

- I AM THANKFUL FOR…   • DATE:
  1.
  2.
  3.

Gratitude unlocks the fullness of life.
What are you grateful for this week?

Gratitude
changes everything.

- I AM THANKFUL FOR···   DATE:
  1.
  2.
  3.

- I AM THANKFUL FOR···   DATE:
  1.
  2.
  3.

- I AM THANKFUL FOR···   DATE:
  1.
  2.
  3.

- I AM THANKFUL FOR...   DATE:
   1.
   2.
   3.

- I AM THANKFUL FOR...   DATE:
   1.
   2.
   3.

- I AM THANKFUL FOR...   DATE:
   1.
   2.
   3.

- I AM THANKFUL FOR...   · DATE:
   1.
   2.
   3.

Gratitude unlocks the fullness of life.
What are you grateful for this week?

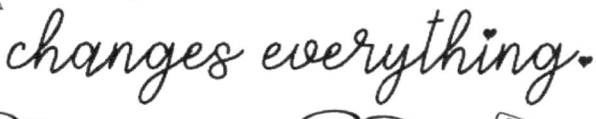

Gratitude
changes everything.

- I AM THANKFUL FOR...   DATE:
    1.
    2.
    3.

- I AM THANKFUL FOR...   DATE:
    1.
    2.
    3.

- I AM THANKFUL FOR...   DATE:
    1.
    2.
    3.

- I AM THANKFUL FOR... DATE:
  1.
  2.
  3.

- I AM THANKFUL FOR... DATE:
  1.
  2.
  3.

- I AM THANKFUL FOR... DATE:
  1.
  2.
  3.

- I AM THANKFUL FOR... • DATE:
  1.
  2.
  3.

Gratitude unlocks the fullness of life.
What are you grateful for this week?

Gratitude
changes everything.

- I AM THANKFUL FOR...   DATE:
  1.
  2.
  3.

- I AM THANKFUL FOR...   DATE:
  1.
  2.
  3.

- I AM THANKFUL FOR...   DATE:
  1.
  2.
  3.

- I AM THANKFUL FOR...   DATE:
1.
2.
3.

- I AM THANKFUL FOR...   DATE:
1.
2.
3.

- I AM THANKFUL FOR...   DATE:
1.
2.
3.

- I AM THANKFUL FOR...   - DATE:
1.
2.
3.

Gratitude unlocks the fullness of life.
What are you grateful for this week?

Gratitude
changes everything.

- I AM THANKFUL FOR...   DATE:
1.
2.
3.

- I AM THANKFUL FOR...   DATE:
1.
2.
3.

- I AM THANKFUL FOR...   DATE:
1.
2.
3.

- I AM THANKFUL FOR...   DATE:
  1.
  2.
  3.

- I AM THANKFUL FOR...   DATE:
  1.
  2.
  3.

- I AM THANKFUL FOR...   DATE:
  1.
  2.
  3.

- I AM THANKFUL FOR...   • DATE:
  1.
  2.
  3.

Gratitude unlocks the fullness of life.
What are you grateful for this week?

Gratitude
changes everything.

- I AM THANKFUL FOR...   DATE:
  1.
  2.
  3.

- I AM THANKFUL FOR...   DATE:
  1.
  2.
  3.

- I AM THANKFUL FOR...   DATE:
  1.
  2.
  3.

- I AM THANKFUL FOR···   DATE:
  1.
  2.
  3.

- I AM THANKFUL FOR···   DATE:
  1.
  2.
  3.

- I AM THANKFUL FOR···   DATE:
  1.
  2.
  3.

- I AM THANKFUL FOR···   • DATE:
  1.
  2.
  3.

Gratitude unlocks the fullness of life.
What are you grateful for this week?

Gratitude
changes everything.

- I AM THANKFUL FOR...   DATE:
  1.
  2.
  3.

- I AM THANKFUL FOR...   DATE:
  1.
  2.
  3.

- I AM THANKFUL FOR...   DATE:
  1.
  2.
  3.

- I AM THANKFUL FOR...   DATE:
1.
2.
3.

- I AM THANKFUL FOR...   DATE:
1.
2.
3.

- I AM THANKFUL FOR...   DATE:
1.
2.
3.

- I AM THANKFUL FOR...   • DATE:
1.
2.
3.

Gratitude unlocks the fullness of life.
What are you grateful for this week?

Gratitude
changes everything.

- **I AM THANKFUL FOR...** DATE:
  1.
  2.
  3.

- **I AM THANKFUL FOR...** DATE:
  1.
  2.
  3.

- **I AM THANKFUL FOR...** DATE:
  1.
  2.
  3.

- I AM THANKFUL FOR... DATE:
  1.
  2.
  3.

- I AM THANKFUL FOR... DATE:
  1.
  2.
  3.

- I AM THANKFUL FOR... DATE:
  1.
  2.
  3.

- I AM THANKFUL FOR... - DATE:
  1.
  2.
  3.

Gratitude unlocks the fullness of life.
What are you grateful for this week?

Gratitude
changes everything.

- I AM THANKFUL FOR…   DATE:
  1.
  2.
  3.

- I AM THANKFUL FOR…   DATE:
  1.
  2.
  3.

- I AM THANKFUL FOR…   DATE:
  1.
  2.
  3.

- I AM THANKFUL FOR…   DATE:
1.
2.
3.

- I AM THANKFUL FOR…   DATE:
1.
2.
3.

- I AM THANKFUL FOR…   DATE:
1.
2.
3.

- I AM THANKFUL FOR…   - DATE:
1.
2.
3.

Gratitude unlocks the fullness of life.
What are you grateful for this week?

Gratitude
changes everything.

- I AM THANKFUL FOR...   DATE:
    1.
    2.
    3.

- I AM THANKFUL FOR...   DATE:
    1.
    2.
    3.

- I AM THANKFUL FOR...   DATE:
    1.
    2.
    3.

- I AM THANKFUL FOR···   DATE:
1.
2.
3.

- I AM THANKFUL FOR···   DATE:
1.
2.
3.

- I AM THANKFUL FOR···   DATE:
1.
2.
3.

- I AM THANKFUL FOR···   - DATE:
1.
2.
3.

Gratitude unlocks the fullness of life.
What are you grateful for this week?

Gratitude
changes everything.

- **I AM THANKFUL FOR···**   DATE:
  1.
  2.
  3.

- **I AM THANKFUL FOR···**   DATE:
  1.
  2.
  3.

- **I AM THANKFUL FOR···**   DATE:
  1.
  2.
  3.

- I AM THANKFUL FOR ···   DATE:
1.
2.
3.

- I AM THANKFUL FOR ···   DATE:
1.
2.
3.

- I AM THANKFUL FOR ···   DATE:
1.
2.
3.

- I AM THANKFUL FOR ···   - DATE:
1.
2.
3.

Gratitude unlocks the fullness of life.
What are you grateful for this week?

Gratitude
changes everything

- I AM THANKFUL FOR…   DATE:
  1.
  2.
  3.

- I AM THANKFUL FOR…   DATE:
  1.
  2.
  3.

- I AM THANKFUL FOR…   DATE:
  1.
  2.
  3.

- I AM THANKFUL FOR··· DATE:
  1.
  2.
  3.

- I AM THANKFUL FOR··· DATE:
  1.
  2.
  3.

- I AM THANKFUL FOR··· DATE:
  1.
  2.
  3.

- I AM THANKFUL FOR··· • DATE:
  1.
  2.
  3.

Gratitude unlocks the fullness of life.
What are you grateful for this week?

Gratitude
changes everything.

- I AM THANKFUL FOR…   DATE:
    1.
    2.
    3.

- I AM THANKFUL FOR…   DATE:
    1.
    2.
    3.

- I AM THANKFUL FOR…   DATE:
    1.
    2.
    3.

- I AM THANKFUL FOR...   DATE:
  1.
  2.
  3.

- I AM THANKFUL FOR...   DATE:
  1.
  2.
  3.

- I AM THANKFUL FOR...   DATE:
  1.
  2.
  3.

- I AM THANKFUL FOR...   ▪ DATE:
  1.
  2.
  3.

Gratitude unlocks the fullness of life.
What are you grateful for this week?

Gratitude
changes everything.

- I AM THANKFUL FOR...   DATE:
    1.
    2.
    3.

- I AM THANKFUL FOR...   DATE:
    1.
    2.
    3.

- I AM THANKFUL FOR...   DATE:
    1.
    2.
    3.

- I AM THANKFUL FOR···   DATE:
  1.
  2.
  3.

- I AM THANKFUL FOR···   DATE:
  1.
  2.
  3.

- I AM THANKFUL FOR···   DATE:
  1.
  2.
  3.

- I AM THANKFUL FOR···   • DATE:
  1.
  2.
  3.

Gratitude unlocks the fullness of life.
What are you grateful for this week?

Gratitude
changes everything.

- I AM THANKFUL FOR... DATE:
1.
2.
3.

- I AM THANKFUL FOR... DATE:
1.
2.
3.

- I AM THANKFUL FOR... DATE:
1.
2.
3.

- I AM THANKFUL FOR...   DATE:
1.
2.
3.

- I AM THANKFUL FOR...   DATE:
1.
2.
3.

- I AM THANKFUL FOR...   DATE:
1.
2.
3.

- I AM THANKFUL FOR...   • DATE:
1.
2.
3.

Gratitude unlocks the fullness of life.
What are you grateful for this week?

Gratitude
changes everything.

- I AM THANKFUL FOR···   DATE:
  1.
  2.
  3.

- I AM THANKFUL FOR···   DATE:
  1.
  2.
  3.

- I AM THANKFUL FOR···   DATE:
  1.
  2.
  3.

- I AM THANKFUL FOR...   DATE:
1.
2.
3.

- I AM THANKFUL FOR...   DATE:
1.
2.
3.

- I AM THANKFUL FOR...   DATE:
1.
2.
3.

- I AM THANKFUL FOR...   • DATE:
1.
2.
3.

Gratitude unlocks the fullness of life.
What are you grateful for this week?

Gratitude
changes everything

- I AM THANKFUL FOR...   DATE:
    1.
    2.
    3.

- I AM THANKFUL FOR...   DATE:
    1.
    2.
    3.

- I AM THANKFUL FOR...   DATE:
    1.
    2.
    3.

- I AM THANKFUL FOR ···   DATE:
  1.
  2.
  3.

- I AM THANKFUL FOR ···   DATE:
  1.
  2.
  3.

- I AM THANKFUL FOR ···   DATE:
  1.
  2.
  3.

- I AM THANKFUL FOR ···   - DATE:
  1.
  2.
  3.

Gratitude unlocks the fullness of life.
What are you grateful for this week?

Gratitude
changes everything.

- **I AM THANKFUL FOR...**   DATE:
  1.
  2.
  3.

- **I AM THANKFUL FOR...**   DATE:
  1.
  2.
  3.

- **I AM THANKFUL FOR...**   DATE:
  1.
  2.
  3.

- I AM THANKFUL FOR...   DATE:
1.
2.
3.

- I AM THANKFUL FOR...   DATE:
1.
2.
3.

- I AM THANKFUL FOR...   DATE:
1.
2.
3.

- I AM THANKFUL FOR...   - DATE:
1.
2.
3.

Gratitude unlocks the fullness of life.
What are you grateful for this week?

Gratitude
changes everything.

- I AM THANKFUL FOR…   DATE:
  1.
  2.
  3.

- I AM THANKFUL FOR…   DATE:
  1.
  2.
  3.

- I AM THANKFUL FOR…   DATE:
  1.
  2.
  3.

- I AM THANKFUL FOR…   DATE:
  1.
  2.
  3.

- I AM THANKFUL FOR…   DATE:
  1.
  2.
  3.

- I AM THANKFUL FOR…   DATE:
  1.
  2.
  3.

- I AM THANKFUL FOR…   • DATE:
  1.
  2.
  3.

Gratitude unlocks the fullness of life.
What are you grateful for this week?

Gratitude
changes everything

- **I AM THANKFUL FOR...** DATE:
  1.
  2.
  3.

- **I AM THANKFUL FOR...** DATE:
  1.
  2.
  3.

- **I AM THANKFUL FOR...** DATE:
  1.
  2.
  3.

- I AM THANKFUL FOR···   DATE:
1.
2.
3.

- I AM THANKFUL FOR···   DATE:
1.
2.
3.

- I AM THANKFUL FOR···   DATE:
1.
2.
3.

- I AM THANKFUL FOR···   - DATE:
1.
2.
3.

Gratitude unlocks the fullness of life.
What are you grateful for this week?

Gratitude
changes everything.

- I AM THANKFUL FOR…   DATE:
    1.
    2.
    3.

- I AM THANKFUL FOR…   DATE:
    1.
    2.
    3.

- I AM THANKFUL FOR…   DATE:
    1.
    2.
    3.

- I AM THANKFUL FOR ⋯   DATE:
   1.
   2.
   3.

- I AM THANKFUL FOR ⋯   DATE:
   1.
   2.
   3.

- I AM THANKFUL FOR ⋯   DATE:
   1.
   2.
   3.

- I AM THANKFUL FOR ⋯   • DATE:
   1.
   2.
   3.

Gratitude unlocks the fullness of life.
What are you grateful for this week?

Gratitude
changes everything.

- I AM THANKFUL FOR...   DATE:
  1.
  2.
  3.

- I AM THANKFUL FOR...   DATE:
  1.
  2.
  3.

- I AM THANKFUL FOR...   DATE:
  1.
  2.
  3.

- I AM THANKFUL FOR ··· DATE:
  1.
  2.
  3.

- I AM THANKFUL FOR ··· DATE:
  1.
  2.
  3.

- I AM THANKFUL FOR ··· DATE:
  1.
  2.
  3.

- I AM THANKFUL FOR ··· • DATE:
  1.
  2.
  3.

Gratitude unlocks the fullness of life.
What are you grateful for this week?

Gratitude
changes everything.

- I AM THANKFUL FOR...   DATE:

1.
2.
3.

- I AM THANKFUL FOR...   DATE:

1.
2.
3.

- I AM THANKFUL FOR...   DATE:

1.
2.
3.

- I AM THANKFUL FOR ⋯   DATE:
  1.
  2.
  3.

- I AM THANKFUL FOR ⋯   DATE:
  1.
  2.
  3.

- I AM THANKFUL FOR ⋯   DATE:
  1.
  2.
  3.

- I AM THANKFUL FOR ⋯   • DATE:
  1.
  2.
  3.

Gratitude unlocks the fullness of life.
What are you grateful for this week?

Gratitude
changes everything.

- I AM THANKFUL FOR…   DATE:
  1.
  2.
  3.

- I AM THANKFUL FOR…   DATE:
  1.
  2.
  3.

- I AM THANKFUL FOR…   DATE:
  1.
  2.
  3.

- I AM THANKFUL FOR...   DATE:
  1.
  2.
  3.

- I AM THANKFUL FOR...   DATE:
  1.
  2.
  3.

- I AM THANKFUL FOR...   DATE:
  1.
  2.
  3.

- I AM THANKFUL FOR...   • DATE:
  1.
  2.
  3.

Gratitude unlocks the fullness of life.
What are you grateful for this week?

Gratitude
changes everything

- I AM THANKFUL FOR...   DATE:
  1.
  2.
  3.

- I AM THANKFUL FOR...   DATE:
  1.
  2.
  3.

- I AM THANKFUL FOR...   DATE:
  1.
  2.
  3.

- I AM THANKFUL FOR...   DATE:
    1.
    2.
    3.

- I AM THANKFUL FOR...   DATE:
    1.
    2.
    3.

- I AM THANKFUL FOR...   DATE:
    1.
    2.
    3.

- I AM THANKFUL FOR...   • DATE:
    1.
    2.
    3.

Gratitude unlocks the fullness of life. What are you grateful for this week?

Gratitude
changes everything.

- **I AM THANKFUL FOR...**   DATE:
    1.
    2.
    3.

- **I AM THANKFUL FOR...**   DATE:
    1.
    2.
    3.

- **I AM THANKFUL FOR...**   DATE:
    1.
    2.
    3.

- I AM THANKFUL FOR...   DATE:
  1.
  2.
  3.

- I AM THANKFUL FOR...   DATE:
  1.
  2.
  3.

- I AM THANKFUL FOR...   DATE:
  1.
  2.
  3.

- I AM THANKFUL FOR...   • DATE:
  1.
  2.
  3.

Gratitude unlocks the fullness of life.
What are you grateful for this week?

Gratitude
changes everything.

- I AM THANKFUL FOR…   DATE:
   1.
   2.
   3.

- I AM THANKFUL FOR…   DATE:
   1.
   2.
   3.

- I AM THANKFUL FOR…   DATE:
   1.
   2.
   3.

- I AM THANKFUL FOR···   DATE:
  1.
  2.
  3.

- I AM THANKFUL FOR···   DATE:
  1.
  2.
  3.

- I AM THANKFUL FOR···   DATE:
  1.
  2.
  3.

- I AM THANKFUL FOR···   ▪ DATE:
  1.
  2.
  3.

Gratitude unlocks the fullness of life. What are you grateful for this week?

Gratitude
changes everything.

- **I AM THANKFUL FOR...**   DATE:
  1.
  2.
  3.

- **I AM THANKFUL FOR...**   DATE:
  1.
  2.
  3.

- **I AM THANKFUL FOR...**   DATE:
  1.
  2.
  3.

- I AM THANKFUL FOR...   DATE:
1.
2.
3.

- I AM THANKFUL FOR...   DATE:
1.
2.
3.

- I AM THANKFUL FOR...   DATE:
1.
2.
3.

- I AM THANKFUL FOR...   ▪ DATE:
1.
2.
3.

Gratitude unlocks the fullness of life.
What are you grateful for this week?

Gratitude
changes everything

- **I AM THANKFUL FOR...**   DATE:
    1.
    2.
    3.

- **I AM THANKFUL FOR...**   DATE:
    1.
    2.
    3.

- **I AM THANKFUL FOR...**   DATE:
    1.
    2.
    3.

- I AM THANKFUL FOR··· DATE:
  1.
  2.
  3.

- I AM THANKFUL FOR··· DATE:
  1.
  2.
  3.

- I AM THANKFUL FOR··· DATE:
  1.
  2.
  3.

- I AM THANKFUL FOR··· • DATE:
  1.
  2.
  3.

Gratitude unlocks the fullness of life.
What are you grateful for this week?

Gratitude
changes everything.

- **I AM THANKFUL FOR...**　　　DATE:

    1.
    2.
    3.

- **I AM THANKFUL FOR...**　　　DATE:

    1.
    2.
    3.

- **I AM THANKFUL FOR...**　　　DATE:

    1.
    2.
    3.

- I AM THANKFUL FOR···   DATE:
1.
2.
3.

- I AM THANKFUL FOR···   DATE:
1.
2.
3.

- I AM THANKFUL FOR···   DATE:
1.
2.
3.

- I AM THANKFUL FOR···   - DATE:
1.
2.
3.

Gratitude unlocks the fullness of life.
What are you grateful for this week?

Gratitude
changes everything

- I AM THANKFUL FOR...   DATE:
1.
2.
3.

- I AM THANKFUL FOR...   DATE:
1.
2.
3.

- I AM THANKFUL FOR...   DATE:
1.
2.
3.

- I AM THANKFUL FOR···   DATE:
   1.
   2.
   3.

- I AM THANKFUL FOR···   DATE:
   1.
   2.
   3.

- I AM THANKFUL FOR···   DATE:
   1.
   2.
   3.

- I AM THANKFUL FOR···   - DATE:
   1.
   2.
   3.

Gratitude unlocks the fullness of life.
What are you grateful for this week?

Gratitude
changes everything.

- I AM THANKFUL FOR...   DATE:
  1.
  2.
  3.

- I AM THANKFUL FOR...   DATE:
  1.
  2.
  3.

- I AM THANKFUL FOR...   DATE:
  1.
  2.
  3.

- I AM THANKFUL FOR...   DATE:
    1.
    2.
    3.

- I AM THANKFUL FOR...   DATE:
    1.
    2.
    3.

- I AM THANKFUL FOR...   DATE:
    1.
    2.
    3.

- I AM THANKFUL FOR...   - DATE:
    1.
    2.
    3.

Gratitude unlocks the fullness of life.
What are you grateful for this week?

Gratitude
changes everything.

- I AM THANKFUL FOR...   DATE:
1.
2.
3.

- I AM THANKFUL FOR...   DATE:
1.
2.
3.

- I AM THANKFUL FOR...   DATE:
1.
2.
3.

- I AM THANKFUL FOR…   DATE:
1.
2.
3.

- I AM THANKFUL FOR…   DATE:
1.
2.
3.

- I AM THANKFUL FOR…   DATE:
1.
2.
3.

- I AM THANKFUL FOR…   • DATE:
1.
2.
3.

Gratitude unlocks the fullness of life.
What are you grateful for this week?

Gratitude
changes everything.

- I AM THANKFUL FOR···   DATE:

1.
2.
3.

- I AM THANKFUL FOR···   DATE:

1.
2.
3.

- I AM THANKFUL FOR···   DATE:

1.
2.
3.

- I AM THANKFUL FOR...   DATE:
  1.
  2.
  3.

- I AM THANKFUL FOR...   DATE:
  1.
  2.
  3.

- I AM THANKFUL FOR...   DATE:
  1.
  2.
  3.

- I AM THANKFUL FOR...   • DATE:
  1.
  2.
  3.

Gratitude unlocks the fullness of life.
What are you grateful for this week?

Gratitude
changes everything.

- I AM THANKFUL FOR...   DATE:
    1.
    2.
    3.

- I AM THANKFUL FOR...   DATE:
    1.
    2.
    3.

- I AM THANKFUL FOR...   DATE:
    1.
    2.
    3.

- I AM THANKFUL FOR...   DATE:
1.
2.
3.

- I AM THANKFUL FOR...   DATE:
1.
2.
3.

- I AM THANKFUL FOR...   DATE:
1.
2.
3.

- I AM THANKFUL FOR...   - DATE:
1.
2.
3.

Gratitude unlocks the fullness of life.
What are you grateful for this week?

Gratitude
changes everything.

- I AM THANKFUL FOR...   DATE:
  1.
  2.
  3.

- I AM THANKFUL FOR...   DATE:
  1.
  2.
  3.

- I AM THANKFUL FOR...   DATE:
  1.
  2.
  3.

- I AM THANKFUL FOR...   DATE:
  1.
  2.
  3.

- I AM THANKFUL FOR...   DATE:
  1.
  2.
  3.

- I AM THANKFUL FOR...   DATE:
  1.
  2.
  3.

- I AM THANKFUL FOR...   • DATE:
  1.
  2.
  3.

Gratitude unlocks the fullness of life.
What are you grateful for this week?

Gratitude
changes everything.

- I AM THANKFUL FOR...   DATE:

1.
2.
3.

- I AM THANKFUL FOR...   DATE:

1.
2.
3.

- I AM THANKFUL FOR...   DATE:

1.
2.
3.

- I AM THANKFUL FOR ···   DATE:
   1.
   2.
   3.

- I AM THANKFUL FOR ···   DATE:
   1.
   2.
   3.

- I AM THANKFUL FOR ···   DATE:
   1.
   2.
   3.

- I AM THANKFUL FOR ···   - DATE:
   1.
   2.
   3.

Gratitude unlocks the fullness of life.
What are you grateful for this week?

Gratitude
changes everything.

- I AM THANKFUL FOR···   DATE:
    1.
    2.
    3.

- I AM THANKFUL FOR···   DATE:
    1.
    2.
    3.

- I AM THANKFUL FOR···   DATE:
    1.
    2.
    3.

- I AM THANKFUL FOR...   DATE:
  1.
  2.
  3.

- I AM THANKFUL FOR...   DATE:
  1.
  2.
  3.

- I AM THANKFUL FOR...   DATE:
  1.
  2.
  3.

- I AM THANKFUL FOR...   • DATE:
  1.
  2.
  3.

Gratitude unlocks the fullness of life.
What are you grateful for this week?

Gratitude
changes everything.

- **I AM THANKFUL FOR...**   DATE:
    1.
    2.
    3.

- **I AM THANKFUL FOR...**   DATE:
    1.
    2.
    3.

- **I AM THANKFUL FOR...**   DATE:
    1.
    2.
    3.

- I AM THANKFUL FOR···   DATE:
   1.
   2.
   3.

- I AM THANKFUL FOR···   DATE:
   1.
   2.
   3.

- I AM THANKFUL FOR···   DATE:
   1.
   2.
   3.

- I AM THANKFUL FOR···   • DATE:
   1.
   2.
   3.

Gratitude unlocks the fullness of life.
What are you grateful for this week?

Gratitude
changes everything.

- **I AM THANKFUL FOR···** DATE:
  1.
  2.
  3.

- **I AM THANKFUL FOR···** DATE:
  1.
  2.
  3.

- **I AM THANKFUL FOR···** DATE:
  1.
  2.
  3.

- I AM THANKFUL FOR ...   DATE:
  1.
  2.
  3.

- I AM THANKFUL FOR ...   DATE:
  1.
  2.
  3.

- I AM THANKFUL FOR ...   DATE:
  1.
  2.
  3.

- I AM THANKFUL FOR ...   • DATE:
  1.
  2.
  3.

Gratitude unlocks the fullness of life.
What are you grateful for this week?

Gratitude
changes everything

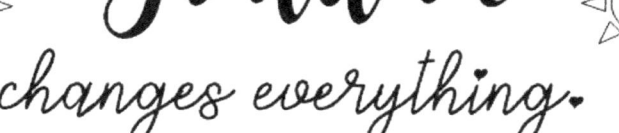

- I AM THANKFUL FOR...   DATE:
  1.
  2.
  3.

- I AM THANKFUL FOR...   DATE:
  1.
  2.
  3.

- I AM THANKFUL FOR...   DATE:
  1.
  2.
  3.

- I AM THANKFUL FOR···   DATE:
1.
2.
3.

- I AM THANKFUL FOR···   DATE:
1.
2.
3.

- I AM THANKFUL FOR···   DATE:
1.
2.
3.

- I AM THANKFUL FOR···   • DATE:
1.
2.
3.

Gratitude unlocks the fullness of life.
What are you grateful for this week?

CPSIA information can be obtained
at www.ICGtesting.com
Printed in the USA
LVHW02s2228100918
589761LV00026B/1294/P